TWO SEPTEMBER

Mac Wellman

BROADWAY PLAY PUBLISHING INC
224 E 62nd St, NY, NY 10065
www.broadwayplaypub.com
info@broadwayplaypub.com

TWO SEPTEMBER
© Copyright 2008 by Mac Wellman

First printing: December 2008
I S B N: 0-88145-417-6

Book design: Marie Donovan
Word processing: Microsoft Word
Typographic controls: Ventura Publisher
Typeface: Palatino
Printed and bound in the U S A

TWO SEPTEMBER was originally produced by the Flea Theater in New York City; the first performance was on 29 November 2006. The cast and creative contributors were:

JOSEPHINE HERBST .... Jayne Haynes
FIRST O S S OFFICER .... Christian Baskous
SECOND O S S OFFICER .... Drew Hildebrand
HO CHI MINH .... Arthur Acuña
THREE COLORS .. Sarah Sirota, Sarah Silk & Annie Scott

Director. .... Loy Arcenas
Lighting design .... Ben Stanton
Costume design Oana Botez-Ban
Sound design .... Leah Gelpe
Stage manager .... Lindsay Stares

CHARACTERS & SETTING

JOSEPHINE HERBST, *an American writer*
FIRST O S S OFFICER
SECOND O S S OFFICER, *American intelligence officers in Southeast Asia and China, in 1945*
HO CHI MINH, *previously Nguyen Ai Quoc, a Vietnamese revolutionary leader*
EMPEROR BAO DAI *and several other Vietnamese; and the three colors of the glorious flag of France*

The action of the play takes places in various places in China and Vietnam, before and after the Japanese coup of 9 March 1945.

Parts of this play have been adapted from the following: *Why Viet Nam?* by Archimedes Patti and *Vietnam 1945* by David Marr; also, Elinor Langer's biography of Josephine Herbst, and the latter's *New Green World*.

NOTE

The occasional appearance of an asterisk in the middle of a speech indicates that the next speech begins to overlap at that point. A double asterisk indicates that a subsequent speech (not the one immediately following) begins to overlap at that point. The overlapping speeches are all clearly marked in the text.

No one can dig up a hole.
American proverb

alpha

(We see and hear JOSEPHINE HERBST.*)*

JOSEPHINE HERBST: My name is Josephine Herbst.
You wouldn't necessarily have heard of me unless
you are interested in what used to be called "the left".
I mean the "old" left. Remember that? Oh, I knew all
the famous writers of my time. They were my friends.
Ernest Hemingway. Nathanael West. Katherine Anne
Porter.... I spent my whole life working on behalf of
the common man, and woman. I wrote novels too, and
quite a lot of journalism. What I stood for is out of
fashion now, socialism. But all this can change on the
turn of a dime. And I know it will, because that is the
way history works. Take the tyranny of the apparently
triumphant. I am referring to the overproduction of
virtually everything. Because it so happens that often,
what is apparently triumphant runs out of steam.
In fact, truth, justice and a humane social order are
bound to replace the apparently triumphant if it is
not based on truth, justice, and a humane social order.
Sounds quite simple and it is.
  I wouldn't talk this way, but the author of this little
drama obviously feels a little intimidated to take on
me and my time, and no wonder. Some day my books
will be read again, and people will see just how true
they are and, well, just how god damn well-made.
I recommend the trilogy to start, *Pity Is Not Enough*,
The Executioner Awaits and *Rope Of Gold*. After that
it is up to you.
  Now back in 1942, when America finally got involved
in the war against fascism...Pearl Harbor, surely some

of your remember that? I had gone to Washington
to get a job with the war effort. Archibald MacLeish
had gathered a group of writers to become engaged
with the government's information program, the
Office of Facts and Figures. Somehow I ended up
instead employed at the Office of the Coordinator of
Information, which was also known as the Donovan
Committee, after its director, William J Donovan.

Eventually this outfit merged activities with those
of the Office of Strategic Services, run by a bunch
of mandarin Yalies; men like James Jesus Angleton.
Finally it became the Central Intelligence Agency,
and we all know what that is.... I worked in the foreign
radio operations section, run by Robert Sherwood, the
playwright. I was on the German desk, and I worked
on radio scripts for daily broadcast to occupied Europe.
"Now it is my job to undermine what is left of the
German will to live," I wrote in my diary, somewhat
optimistically, as it turned out, since 1945 and V E Day
proved some three years off. But the House Un-
American Affairs Committee, led by Martin Dies had
decided to focus on who was, and who was not, fit to
serve the American cause. For instance, lots of radicals
who had supported, and in many cases fought for
Republican Spain were criticized and subjected to
tough scrutiny. Malcolm Cowley had been driven
out of MacLeish's Office of Facts and Figures along
with someone from the *Herald-Trib* whose name I
forget. On May 21, 1942 I had only been working
on the German desk a few months when I returned
from lunch to find my desk and locker padlocked.
Apparently a grave security risk, I was ushered out
and so spent the remainder of the war back at my house
in Erwinna, Pennsylvania. I was suspected, according
to Robert Sherwood, of being both a communist and a
fascist, something he thought difficult to do at the same
time. In any event, I was not given a precise reason for

my dismissal.

You can't dig up a hole, and history is full of them.

It turns out someone who I thought a good friend had been interviewed by the F B I, at great length, in Reno, Nevada, only a few days before I was excused from public service.

More of this informant later.

Around the time I was trying to sort all this out, and a half a world away, Ho Chi Minh, hoping to improve ties with both the Kuomintang and the Chinese Communist Party crosses the frontier to Kwangsi and is promptly arrested.

By 1944, the Kuomintang General Chang Fa-Kwei has granted him sufficient freedom to spend time at the local U.S. Office of War Information at Kunming. Ho's Viet Minh had helped rescue and return a downed American pilot.

Now to our boys, O S S officers, also in Kunming, China. Same outfit taking care of business back in Washington DC, remember? And the business they are taking care of is processing certain Vietnamese for undercover work in the war effort.

(Lights change.)

FIRST O S S OFFICER: Who's this?

SECOND O S S OFFICER: Who's this who?

FIRST O S S OFFICER: This old Annamite we've been hearing about, Hoo. Not only helped a pilot to escape, but they say is connected to a large political group in Indochina.

(We see HO CHI MINH at a table, reading.)

(Long pause)

FIRST O S S OFFICER: Because I think he's paying us a visit.

SECOND O S S OFFICER: Ho Chi Minh is the correct name. If he is who I think he is. He's made a point of doing what he can to attract American attention. Hence the return of the American flyer. What's more—

(High above, a window is blown open.)

(We hear the wind.)

SECOND O S S OFFICER: What's that?

FIRST O S S OFFICER: What's what?

SECOND O S S OFFICER: Never mind. I thought I heard something.

FIRST O S S OFFICER: ?

SECOND O S S OFFICER: Political welfare and advancement of oppressed people here in the orient. That's his agenda.

FIRST O S S OFFICER: Our chief says we didn't rescue the French from German slavery to undermine their empire. Remains to be seen.

SECOND O S S OFFICER: —

(Both stare at HO CHI MINH.*)*

FIRST O S S OFFICER: What's he doing?

SECOND O S S OFFICER: Reading. Reads everything from *Time* magazine to the *Encyclopedia Americana.*

FIRST O S S OFFICER: "Ho Chi Ming" —code name "Lucius".

SECOND O S S OFFICER: Sir, do you mind filling out this questionnaire? Very short questionnaire.

*(*HO CHI MINH *looks at him.)*

HO CHI MINH: Thirty five items?

SECOND O S S OFFICER: Not so short.

FIRST O S S OFFICER: This one's unusual. He doesn't ask for money.

(Pause)

SECOND O S S OFFICER: Ho Chi Minh is the name. Though he also goes by Nguyen Ai Quoc. Also referred to as Comrade Wong, Wang and as Ho Chi Ming, Ho Chi Ching. He's a Vietnamese nationalist. Been in a Chinese jail till recently.

FIRST O S S OFFICER: And now he's out? Why? Why did they let him out?

HO CHI MINH: Excuse me. I am not sure how I am to respond to item number fifteen.

(FIRST O S S OFFICER reads out loud)

FIRSTO S S OFFICER: "Details of Jap or collaborationist participation in gambling, drinking, whoring or other vice."

(Both O S S OFFICERS are puzzled.)

HO CHI MINH: Perhaps this document was prepared for the French, as the behavior described belongs more to them than to us.

SECOND O S S OFFICER: I don't know what to say.

FIRST O S S OFFICER: Neither do I.

SECONDO S S OFFICER: He requested, and was granted an interview with General Chennault.

FIRST O S S OFFICER: ?

SECOND O S S OFFICER: General Claire Chennault, of the Flying Tigers, who gave him a signed photo.

(The FIRST O S S OFFICER whistles softly.)

SECONDO S S OFFICER: And a request for a set of six, brand-new, Colt .45 automatic pistols, as appreciation for his efforts against the Japs.

(Pause)

HO CHI MINH: I'm going back to Pac Bo. With your permission.

SECOND O S S OFFICER: I am deeply impressed by what you have told us, by your sincerity and eloquence. And also by your refusal to exaggerate the strengths of your group.

SECOND O S S OFFICER: Okay. Okay. Send Frank Tan with him. Along with a forty-man armed escort. Twenty-five porter loads of sten guns, Thompson submachine guns and communication gear. Whatever we can acquire from other allied information agencies.

HO CHI MINH: Once we get there we shall carve out an airstrip in the jungle for your L-5 observer craft.

(HO CHI MINH gets up and goes.)

FIRST O S S OFFICER: You can get away with this as long as you stay out of politics. Ha!

SECOND O S S OFFICER: —

(Both laugh.)

(JOSEPHINE HERBST laughs too.)

JOSEPHINE HERBST: As if anyone can stay out of politics ever. Stay out of politics indeed. But this is May 1945 and President Roosevelt, who strongly opposed the reestablishment of French rule in Indochina, has died. President Truman has to face pressure from the old China hands in State, not to mention both Churchill and De Gaulle.

Pressure to undo Roosevelt's policy and bring back the old colonial systems.

Staying out of politics is something politicians only claim to do when they don't want you to know what their politics are.

(JOSEPHINE HERBST *goes out and* HO CHI MINH,
looking very ill, enters and sits.)

(*We are in the jungles of northern Vietnam.*)

(*The* O S S OFFICERS *have been air dropped.*)

(*The* FIRST O S S OFFICER *holds their parachutes.*)

HO CHI MINH: Your statesmen make eloquent speeches
about helping those who need it with
self-determination. We are self-determined. Why not
help us? Am I different from Nehru, Quezon in the
Philippines, even your George Washington? Was not
Washington considered a revolutionary? I want to set
my people free.

FIRST O S S OFFICER: Malaria, dysentery and other
complications.
   With Sulfa drugs and quinine. He'll be as good as
new.

SECONDO S S OFFICER: I'm starting to get a little flack
from Washington. I'm becoming uncertain about your
status. As non-communist or communist or whatever.

HO CHI MINH: We are all united now. We will discuss
politics later.

(*Long pause. They look at each closely.*)

HO CHI MINH: Our hosts are of the Tay ethnic group.
They believe I have worked a miracle.

SECOND O S S OFFICER: Why?

HO CHI MINH: Because I told them to go to a particular
clearing and wait for men "to fall from the sky".

SECONDO S S OFFICER: You can have the parachutes.
You can use them to repair your clothing.

HO CHI MINH: Yes, the clothes are in terrible condition.
But whatever the clothing, we want to make a country
here, one country. That is why we refuse to use terms

from the colonial time. Terms like "Annamite" and "Tonkinese". We are all one people.
  Such terms are more tattered than our clothes.

(Pause)

SECOND O S S OFFICER: You listen to everything we say very, very carefully. Why so carefully?

HO CHI MINH: I want to hear you talk about your history, your political ideals, and how your President Roosevelt has offered official support for free, popular governments all over the world.

(Long pause)

You are from Boston. Did you know I worked there, briefly? As a waiter, in a restaurant.

SECOND O S S OFFICER: At Headquarters, back in Kunming. We are starting to get pressure, from Washington. Not to get involved. The O S S still has cachet. Roosevelt prized our adroitness, but he's gone now.

HO CHI MINH: That is why I want you to talk about your own history. You must remind yourselves that you are a very great nation, and it is a duty of yours to help small nations to determine their own freedom

SECOND O S S OFFICER: De Gaulle has promised you self-government.

(HO CHI MINH just looks at him.)

(Long pause. End of scene)

Beta

(JOSEPHINE HERBST *as before, at the beginning of the play.*)

JOSEPHINE HERBST: By the summer of 1945, Paris received from Kunming a dossier compiled by the Surete in Indochina which established conclusively that Ho Chi Minh was, in fact, none other than Nguyen Ai Quoc, founder of the Indochinese Communist Party and believed dead for thirteen years.

But we already knew that. He was also a founder of the French Communist Party. At Versailles, he was shown the door when he made the mistake of taking seriously Wilson's Fourteen Points, and in particular, the part about guaranteeing independence for the Asian colonies of European powers.

(*Back to our O S S boys as before. The* SECOND O S S OFFICER *has some papers in his hand.*)

SECOND O S S OFFICER: Ho wants me to pass this along to the French Military Mission in Kunming. It calls for an Indochinese parliament elected by universal suffrage, a French governor-general to preside until independence is granted in five to ten years, mutual economic programs, such political freedoms as are specified by the U N Charter, and prohibition of the sale of opium.

FIRST O S S OFFICER: —

(*They stare at each other.*)

(*Pause*)

SECOND O S S OFFICER: I am also instructed to express the Vietnamese readiness to talk with a high ranking French official, either in Kunming or in Kim Lung.

(*The* FIRST O S S OFFICER*other just laughs.*)

SECONDO S S OFFICER: After the Japanese coup in March it was all over for the French. Their "mandate of heaven..."

HO CHI MINH: *(Off)* ...*thien menh...*

SECOND O S S OFFICER: ...has been revoked.

HO CHI MINH: *(Off)* ...*cach menh...*

SECOND O S S OFFICER: The French don't understand, do they?

FIRST O S S OFFICER: They never will. *(Pause)* We've dropped the atom bomb. The war will be over within days now, not months or another year like everyone was thinking. That's what I call a mandate of heaven.

SECOND O S S OFFICER: All bets are off now.

FIRST O S S OFFICER: We've blown a hole in the fabric of history.

SECOND O S S OFFICER: It's what the Vietnamese call an "opportune moment". A "favorable occasion".

HO CHI MINH: *(From off again)* ...*thoi co; co hoi...* *(Now he comes down and reads us a letter.)* Dear Lieutenant,
   The war is finished. It is good for every body. I feel only sorry

that all our American friends have to leave us so soon. And their leaving this country means that relations between you and us will be more difficult.
   The war is won. But we small and subject countries have no share, or very small share, in the victory of freedom and democracy. Probably, if we want to get a sufficient share, we have still to fight. I believe that your sympaty and the sympaty of the great American people will be always with us.
   I also remain sure that sooner or later, we will attain our aim because it is just. And our country get

independent, I am looking forward for the happy day
of meeting you and our other American friend either
in Indo-China or in the U S A!

I wish you good luck & good health,

(HO CHI MINH *fades out as light come up on the two O S S
men. They have the letter before them.*)

FIRST O S S OFFICER: Signed: C M Hoo.

Oh, and guess who's trying to hitch a ride with us
when we fly into Hanoi? Jean Sainteny, the French
Mission officer here in Kunming. And, get this, now
that the flight's been postponed because of the heavy
rainfall he's going around accusing us of sabotaging
his mission.

SECOND O S S OFFICER: There's been a big
demonstration in Hanoi, as many as two hundred
thousand people gathered in front of the opera house.
Speakers announced: "Following orders from the
Emperor, the Japanese have ceased fighting on all
fronts."

FIRST O S S OFFICER: But I hear the Japs won't surrender
to the Vietnamese, They say to them, we won't
surrender to you because you never defeated us, the
allies did. They won't even turn over their weapons.

SECOND O S S OFFICER: They've got a point there, but
it could take weeks before General Order Number 1,
on surrender dispositions can even begin to be carried
out. In the meantime, the Japanese are pretty much in
charge, as they were before.

FIRST O S S OFFICER: As if the war never ended.

(*Lights down on them, and up on:*)

JOSEPHINE HERBST: Back in Washington, after I was
let go, I made some efforts to discover the exact nature
of the charges against me. Colonel Donovan, who had
ordered my dismissal was, shall we say, uncooperative.

Robert Sherwood was sympathetic, but what could he
do? The matter was out of his hands. My friends stood
firmly by me. Katherine Anne, for instance, said she
was horrified and I believe she was. *(Pause)* Several
weeks later I did manage to get some idea of what was
in the various anonymous accusations, including the
longest and most extraordinary of these, the Reno
number, and what it came down to was, in its own way,
remarkable. I was "reported" to have been a
"pre-mature anti-fascist, that is, a person hostile to
Germany before the Nazi-Soviet Pact of 1939; I was
"reported"

to have supported the Communist ticket of Browder
and Ford in 1936; I was "reported" to have contributed
to a banquet honoring Mother Bloor, et cetera. *(Pause)* "I
am reported," I responded, "to have protested against
the violation of various civil liberties...in the thirties.
"I am reported to have printed articles in magazines
known to The Measuring Stick as 'Left'. I am grateful
that during the last decade I was not confined to the
Saturday Evening Post for expression.

I am reported to have been actively interested in the
Loyalist cause in Spain, but in order to damn me they
allege that I had taken part in a Communist Party
broadcast from Spain.... My answer is: I would have
broadcast from Spain under any auspices, including
the Communist Party, in order to have one tiny chance
of arousing people in England, France, and in the U S A
to the danger that threatened not only Spain, but
themselves. History vindicates this position. *(Pause)*
Somehow this has to be brought out of the frame that
the Civil Service has put around it.

Nothing sounds right within that frame. Everything
is warped from its context. Actually now I see I'm on
the stand for trying to be truthful all along. The actual
communists would never have put themselves in such
vulnerable positions. I always expected truth somehow

to prevail and in the end it doubtless does. But in a
session such as this, how can it? As I indicated to the
examiners, it would be necessary to write a book to
make the beginnings of understanding the truth, to
interpret the workings of even one individual in a time
so complicated as the time since the first world war
and this.

How is one to make people understand?

Why is reaching out a hand, not to conspirators about
to throw over a government but to such people as I
knew them, doing this thing or that, defending labor
or fighting fascism...why is that a criminal act? What
is involved in all this? Why are General Motors who
deliberately preached Naziism in Lansing, Michigan
during the last decade never investigated along such
angles or the many people here in Washington DC
whose one virtue has been caution and selfishness and
therefore are fit delegates for fascism once it swept
before the winds?

The measuring stick. That is the place to quarrel, not
with defending myself at all. They cannot accuse me
of acknowledged acts which I shall not allow myself
to regret. *(Pause)* I was unable to write. My only source
of income the rent on the Erwinna house. I traveled,
first to friends in Chicago. Later I traveled west by
myself, I had to be alone with my thoughts. Home
in Sioux City. Seattle. San Francisco. Finally I had to
relocate to Erwinna, on the advice of my lawyers.
My former husband John was trying to have me
evicted, and claim the property for himself.

There was no toilet, there was no tap water, there was
no heat apart from the wood fires I, and a young writer
who came to live with me, could provide. The title of
the property remained unresolved by war's end.

Just after the Allied invasion, I had written in my
journal: D-day at last. Rejoicing reported in Russia.
Calm in London. General de Gaulle may land on the

coast of France. Here the woodchuck ate my morning glories from my fencing for lettuce...June 9, rain in the garden.

(Black out. End of scene)

gamma

(Our boys [O S S] in Hanoi, listening to incoming messages on the radio. What they hear is both complex and confusing. In the background, we hear crowd noise and see a large Viet Minh flag draped on the upstage wall. SECOND O S S OFFICER *begins his own brief transmission.)*

SECOND O S S OFFICER: August 22. As we entered Hanoi, I observed there were no French flags anywhere—only red flags with the five pointed yellow star of the Viet Minh. At the airport the Japanese major in command invited us to a nearby building where we were offered iced towels and cold beer. Later a delegate of the Hanoi City Committee greeted us. In response to his questions I replied that no, I did not anticipate the arrival of French troops; yes, there would be additional Americans coming shortly; yes, it was true I had met President Ho Chi Minh; and no, the United States does not support colonialism...

(The transmission breaks off.)

SECOND O S S OFFICER: Did that go through? Damn.

FIRST O S S OFFICER: Poor Sainteny. One of his men was caught by the Japanese trying to slip into the city on his own. What kind of a welcome did he imagine he would receive there? Sucker...

SECOND O S S OFFICER: *(Transmitting again)* Banners everywhere, in English, Vietnamese, French, Chinese, and Russian: "Independence or death", "Long live

Vietnamese independence", "Death to French imperialism", "Welcome to the Allies",

and "Hurrah for the Allied countries arriving to liberate us". *(Pause)* At the Hotel Metropole we dropped off Sainteny and his colleagues where they met with a group of French civilians who joyously greet Sainteny as their liberator, recount their sad tales of internment, and the killing of Frenchmen by the barbaric Japanese and Annamites. Only a line of bayonet-wielding Japanese holds back a crowd of hostile Vietnamese who occupy themselves with chanting anti-imperialist slogans. *(Pause)* Vietnamese strong and belligerent and definitely anti-French. Suggest no more French be permitted to enter French-Indochina and especially not armed. That's all for now. *(Signs off)*

FIRST O S S OFFICER: Get a load of this.

(Hands a Vietnamese newspaper to his colleague, who reads it aloud.)

SECOND O S S OFFICER: "Viet Minh fighting alongside U S troops in Tonkin Will Soon Be Here to Oust the French Oppressors Who Last Year Starved Two Million People".

FIRST O S S OFFICER: And, furthermore, they quote you here: "...the independence of Viet Nam is quite clear already; it simply needs to be consolidated". Don't you think, maybe you've given them the wrong impression of our policy?

SECOND O S S OFFICER: We're supposed to have some latitude, and as I understand it, this is President Roosevelt's policy.

FIRST O S S OFFICER: President Roosevelt has been dead five months. We have to be more careful.

SECOND O S S OFFICER: I can imagine what kind of reports Sainteny will be sending to Kunming. I received this intercepted message just now from the Japanese liaison officer: it is a complaint against us, the O S S in general, for engineering "a concerted Allied maneuver aimed at eliminating the French in Indochina". He warns of a "total loss of face" for France.

(But the FIRST O S S OFFICER *is not listening. He has seen something he cannot believe: three young French women walk slowly downstage to much cheering. One is dressed in blue, the middle in white, and the third in red. It is a sentimental act of French patriotism in Hanoi.)*

SECOND O S S OFFICER: That's the first time I've seen a French flag since we've arrived.

FIRST O S S OFFICER: Sainteny would say, if he were here: "Yes, *mon ami*, but I give you my word it will not be the last." *(Pause)* You know what? I heard this is the first time Ho Chi Minh has ever set foot in Hanoi. For three decades he's traveled around the world. Been to Paris, New York even. But never here, a hundred and twenty miles from where he grew up in Nhe An province.

(Silence. We hear the wind blow. Silence)

(Pause)

(Both O S S OFFICERS *become thoughtful and very still.)*

SECOND O S S OFFICER: What's that?

FIRST O S S OFFICER: What? What's that?

SECOND O S S OFFICER: I don't know. Thought I heard something. *(Pause)* I don't know what I'm supposed to say now.

FIRST O S S OFFICER: How's that?

SECOND O S S OFFICER: Skip it. Just a little distracted.

FIRST O S S OFFICER: Probably the fatigue.

(Wind blows, fluttering a white cotton curtain, very high up. Both look, see the window is open.)

SECOND O S S OFFICER: Hey, what's that?

(FIRST O S S OFFICER gets up.)

(Pause)

SECOND O S S OFFICER: Are you going to close the window?

FIRST O S S OFFICER: —

SECOND O S S OFFICER: I said: are you going to close the window?
   Look, close the window.

(FIRST O S S OFFICER snaps out of it, and finds a long pole with a brass tipped stud at one end. He goes to the window and closes it. Replaces the pole where he found it. Pause)

(He stands quietly in the shadows.)

SECOND O S S OFFICER: What are you doing? Why are you just standing there? (Pause) Hey! Did you hear what I said? Respond.

FIRST O S S OFFICER: For a minute I had the strangest sensation, as if I didn't know how to speak. As if something had taken my voice.

SECOND O S S OFFICER: Oh, and I'm invited to lunch with them. Ho and some others (He reads): Vo Nguyen Giap, Truongh Chinh, and our liaison with the Viet Minh, Le Xuan. Next Sunday, the 26th.

(Pause. The FIRST O S S OFFICER stares blankly off.)

SECOND O S S OFFICER: I'll need a clean uniform. Maybe you could arrange that?

(The FIRST O S S OFFICER snaps to attention.)

FIRST O S S OFFICER: Yes, sir.

(FIRST O S S OFFICER *salutes in a highly formal way and relaxes visibly. The* SECOND O S S OFFICER *looks hard at him. He goes out.*)

(*Something odd happens. The high window opens and closes all by itself.*)

(HO CHI MINH *enters, looking ill.*)

(*Pause*)

(HO CHI MINH *approaches* SECOND O S S OFFICER *and sits with him.*)

(*They look at each other or a long time.*)

HO CHI MINH: Perhaps you can tell me why Sainteny, the head of the French intelligence operations in China, is now in Hanoi through the good offices of the Americans?

SECOND O S S OFFICER: I admire your frankness.

HO CHI MINH: —

SECOND O S S OFFICER: The French are here to minister to the needs of their P O Ws.

HO CHI MINH: That may be your purpose, but it is not theirs.

SECOND O S S OFFICER: They are concerned, somehow, in some small way, to save face.

(*Pause*)

HO CHI MINH: To save face.

SECOND O S S OFFICER: Precisely, to save face.

(*Pause.* HO CHI MINH *tosses some papers on the table between them.*)

HO CHI MINH: In the accounts I have read in our press, you are said to have reported: a) the French have no role in discussion between the Allies and Japanese in

Indochina; b) the Allies are not assisting or authorizing French military return; c) the United States is well aware that Vietnam is a civilized country, not barbaric as still thought by some and hence incapable of self-government; and d) when the official Allied mission arrives to accept the Japanese surrender Vietnamese citizens ought to mount peaceable demonstrations demanding independence.

(Pause)

SECOND O S S OFFICER: Ought *to be able* to mount peaceable demonstrations, is probably a more accurate statement of my intentions.

HO CHI MINH: This morning, at the parade, my colleague, Vo Nguyen Giap, in bidding farewell to you mentioned, if you remember correctly, that this was the first time in the history of Viet Nam that our flag has been displayed in an international ceremony, and our national anthem played in honor of a foreign guest.

SECOND O S S OFFICER: The O S S has been the creation of President Roosevelt, and its officers in the field have some leeway to interpret central instructions creatively.

(Pause)

HO CHI MINH: My overriding concern is that the French, British and Chinese in tandem may jeopardize the independence of Viet Nam.

SECOND O S S OFFICER: I can promise you everything in the way of my personal support.

HO CHI MINH: Your personal support only?

(The wind suddenly blows open the high window which had been shut. The SECOND O S S OFFICER is startled. HO CHI MINH does not notice at all. Indeed, his focus remains tightly on the SECOND O S S OFFICER.)

(After a few seconds, the FIRST O S S OFFICER *reenters and using the pole as before manages to shut the window. Once more he replaces it as before, and stands at ease in the shadows.*

Pause. Gradually the SECOND O S S OFFICER *and* HO CHI MINH *relax.)*

SECOND O S S OFFICER: You have my personal support, and—as far as I know at this time—the support of the government of the United States.

HO CHI MINH: Very well. *(Rising)*

SECOND O S S OFFICER: I am pledged to convey any message you may have for my superiors in China, and —in Washington—; where I am sure they will be treated expeditiously.

HO CHI MINH: My lieutenants are concerned that my movements may have monitored by the Japanese security forces, the Kempeitai.

SECOND O S S OFFICER: Clearly the Kempeitai are aware both of your whereabouts, and your movements.

HO CHI MINH: Then I am correct in assuming that the Japanese have no reason to forcibly intervene?

SECOND O S S OFFICER: That is our information. As for the French, it might be appropriate if the Viet Minh attempts to establish a direct contact with them.

HO CHI MINH: That is out of the question.

SECOND O S S OFFICER: I would be willing to assist negotiations in any way possible.

HO CHI MINH: We intend to declare, by proclamation, our independence on September 2nd. There is no need to request permission from the French colonialists, nor in any way to suggest that we desire their approval.

SECOND O S S OFFICER: I understand. I understand.

HO CHI MINH: —

SECOND O S S OFFICER: Perhaps it might be more appropriate if one of your colleagues, perhaps Vo Nguyen Giap, met in my presence with the French. I know Sainteny.

HO CHI MINH: I do not like the idea.

SECOND O S S OFFICER: I have spent time with Sainteny. Believe me, he is painfully aware that the situation is extremely fluid. He knows too he possesses no authority from Paris to negotiate anything.

HO CHI MINH: I still do not like the idea.

SECOND O S S OFFICER: The French know you plan to announce a provisional government. Sainteny wants simply to lecture you, says he would be keeping "a watchful eye". Giap would be a good choice. Sainteny considers him "one of the most brilliant products of our culture".

HO CHI MINH: "Our culture", indeed.

(*Both laugh lightly and the* FIRST O S S OFFICER *moves from foot to foot.*)

HO CHI MINH: Very well. You can arrange the meeting.

SECOND O S S OFFICER: I'll get right on it. With your permission.

HO CHI MINH: You have my permission. Even if the support you offer is not what it seemed when we first talked, and when I met the other major and O S S Deer Team at Pac Bo.

SECOND O S S OFFICER: I have always conveyed my respect for your informality, frankness, political sophistication and knowledge of current events in my dispatches to my superiors.

HO CHI MINH: Then I thank you very much for your continued support, especially as it is personal.

(HO CHI MINH bows. The SECOND O S S OFFICER also bows. HO CHI MINH slowly makes his way out, and we realize once more he is a far from healthy man.)

(Slow fade to black)

(Lights up slowly on)

JOSEPHINE HERBST: For a few years I stayed out of politics; made that conscious, if laughable decision. I did a great deal of research, and did a book on the life and times of John Bartram, the eighteenth century American botanist. *New Green World* it was called, and everyone, including myself, was surprised by how successful it was.
(She quotes from memory:)
   The little coterie of men who devoted their lives to what was known as natural history, for it included stones and turtles as well as trees and flowers, were whole men confronting a whole world, not human beings floating in a cultural medium. When a man said "I" he meant exactly "I", not an ego, or superego lost in a soup of determinants. The mistake about the "I" only came later when by saying "I" one meant nothing but one's own fragmented self alone in a world divided into pieces, abstract and aloof. *(Pause)* Who knows the exact origin of a book? A book begins with a writer's "I" even when the matter involves lives that seem disrelated in time and space to his own...
   ...it soon became clear that the ingredient I wished to recover from that vast wilderness so passionately was not only a botanical specimen but the confident lost "I" of whole men.
   These men whose lives I began to explore as Bartram had explored his wilderness seemed closer to stalks of growing grain in the field than we are.
   War and fire might shake the collective field of stalks

but what was left standing could be answered for.
It could be defined. Today the point of gravity for
responsibility has shifted from the small community
to relationships between *things*. Experiences have even
made themselves independent of men. They are to be
found by turning the pages of a pictorial magazine or
in the lazy isolation of one's living room by staring at
the television screen. Over the air ways, in movies,
experiences have come to be dogmatized to certain
kinds of experience at the cost of all others. If
experience does not come from one's actual work
who can say from whence it comes? With so many
people interpreting experience whoever is entitled to
his anger... *(Pause)* ...who even is entitled to his, or her,
anger? The world comes second hand—or fifth
hand—to us and the illusion that it is fresh because
it is shown as a picture of an actual place by some
reporter divides man into incalculable parts without
any true center.

   I wrote that, not any damn spokesman for the
measuring stick.

(Lights down on JOSEPHINE HERBST, *as she walks over to
where our boys in the O S S are seated.)*

(She looks at them. They look at her.)

(She goes out.)

(The SECOND O S S OFFICER *hands something to his
colleague.)*

FIRST O S S OFFICER: ?

SECOND O S S OFFICER: It's his personal calling card,
with a message scrawled today.

FIRST O S S OFFICER: *(Reads aloud)* "Urgent we meet
before noon today. Please come if you can. Hoo."
What on earth do you suppose this is all about?

(Crossfade to Viet Minh H Q.)

(The SECOND O S S OFFICER *is ushered in and seats himself.)*

*(*HO CHI MINH *comes in, unhurried and smiling. He shakes the other's hand in a firm greeting.)*

HO CHI MINH: I was afraid you would not get my message until late in the day. I want very much to talk to you about some of our decisions and future plans. *(Pause)* Tran Van Lieu, who has been received by the Emperor, has shown me the Act of Abdication. It will be read publicly tomorrow, and Bao Dai will turn over the Royal Seal and Sword to a delegation from the Provisional Government. I am elated. This is the end of colonialism as we have known it, and the start of a new era. Although perhaps the struggle is not quite over. *(Pause)* The Chinese are coming, and the French are already here. *(Pause)* But this was not the reason I asked you to come here today. I want you to be the first to know.

SECOND O S S OFFICER: —

HO CHI MINH: On the 27th we convened our first cabinet meeting at the Bac Bo Palace and decided to formalize the Provisional Government and to fix September 2nd as Independence Day. On that occasion we will proclaim the people's independence, present the members of the Provisional Government to the people, and outline the government's program for all to hear.

SECOND O S S OFFICER: I offer you my congratulations, and wish you all success on your great undertaking.

HO CHI MINH: I accept your good wishes, but there is a great deal to accomplish in a very short time. We have a committee that is working right now on the wording of the oath of office I and my officers will pledge. And the draft of our declaration of Independence needs polishing.

(Another man enters with a copy and gives it to HO CHI MINH. *He passes it in turn to the* SECOND O S S OFFICER *with an air of self-satisfaction.)*

(Pause)

(The SECOND O S S OFFICER *looks at the document and then back at* HO CHI MINH *with a little puzzlement.)*

HO CHI MINH: Ah, I had forgotten you do not read Vietnamese.

(He calls for a young assistant who translates for the SECOND O S S OFFICER.*)*

TRANSLATOR: "This immortal statement was made in the Declaration of Independence of the United States of America in 1776".

SECOND O S S OFFICER: Stop. You don't mean to say you intend to put that into your own declaration?

(Slowly HO CHI MINH *sits back in his chair, his palms together with fingertips touching his lips ever so slightly, as though meditating. Pause. He smiles gently.)*

HO CHI MINH: Should I not use it?

SECOND O S S OFFICER: Of course. Of course. Why not. Only for an instant I don't know. I felt nettled. I felt proprietary, and I don't know how to say this.... It's all very inane. Of course you should use it if you feel it is appropriate.

HO CHI MINH: But you reacted as though I should not.

SECOND O S S OFFICER: Now I feel sheepish and embarrassed. Please, use it. We should feel honored that you would be inspired by our own Declaration of Independence. Go on, please. Please. From the top.

*(*HO CHI MINH *studies the* SECOND O S S OFFICER *carefully, and then turns to the young assistant, instructing him to read.*

TRANSLATOR: "All men are created equal; they are endowed by their creator with certain inalienable rights; among these are liberty, life, and the pursuit of happiness".

SECOND O S S OFFICER: Hold it, please. Could you repeat that last part?

HO CHI MINH: Why, is there something wrong?

SECOND O S S OFFICER: There's a mistake there, I believe. If I remember correctly. Could you have your translator repeat that last section?

(Pause)

HO CHI MINH: Certainly.

(HO CHI MINH instructs the assistant to repeat what has just been spoken.

TRANSLATOR: "All men are created equal; they are endowed by their creator with certain inalienable rights; among these are liberty, life and the pursuit of happiness"

SECOND O S S OFFICER: You've got it wrong—you've transposed "liberty" and "life". It should be "life, liberty and the pursuit of happiness. I mean, that's how it goes in the American Declaration of Independence.

HO CHI MINH: Why, of course, there is no liberty without life, and no happiness without liberty. *(He enters the correction into the document himself, and turns back to the* SECOND O S S OFFICER.) You must help us. Are there any more places where we have made similar mistakes? Please, it is an important matter. It is essential that the meaning of the document be as accurate and truthful as possible. Please, you must help us.

SECOND O S S OFFICER: That's it. Really. Believe me. I know nothing about constitutional law. Or anything related to the law. Really. It's true. I am completely ignorant. That's the only part I happen to be familiar with.

And anyway I am becoming a little uncomfortable. I mean, this is your declaration of independence and I'm not sure it's right for me to be involved—even if slightly—in the formulation, ah...of a political entity.

(Pause)

HO CHI MINH: Never mind then.

(Pause. Silence. Pause)

(The SECOND O S S OFFICER *rises to make his departure, and* HO CHI MINH *rises also to bid him farewell.)*

HO CHI MINH: Would you do us the honor of attending a brief ceremony with me on Independence Day?

SECOND O S S OFFICER: Of course. Of course. Although I may not be able to attend. It depends on circumstances, and...and well...it may not be appropriate.

HO CHI MINH: I understand. I understand fully. However, you will be welcome if you are able to attend.

(Slow black)

(End of scene)

delta

(A man appears, very regal and serene, before a podium. He begins to give a speech [everyone will think it is HO CHI MINH, *as we cannot see his face clearly]; it is the Emperor,* BAO DAI's *abdication. After he gets a little way into it,* JOSEPHINE HERBST *appears and focus falls on her, as the speaker and his speech fade out.)*

JOSEPHINE HERBST: That's the Emperor, and Japanese puppet, Bao Dai—not Ho Chi Minh. A few weeks ago he was proud to acknowledge Japan's help in Viet Nam in regaining independence. Using the flowery language of the Confucian literary tradition, he has just abdicated. There is some routine self-chastisement for his inability to drive out the Japanese fascists, along with an attempt to place himself, proudly, in the current patriotic and populist context. Don't worry, in a few months he'll be back, as a French puppet, in a rather nifty move to deny the Democratic Republic of Viet Nam and Ho Chi Minh any legitimacy whatsoever.

History is a threadbare fabric. As full of holes, tears and rents as the clothes of the impoverished people our boys encountered in July at Ho's headquarters near Kim Lung.

And a history, as a thing written, needs to have a start. What makes these times in Vietnam in the summer of 1945 so difficult to grasp, is that one order or system was ending, at least as a legitimate political entity; and another one was just beginning.

In *New Green World* I wrote of the Bartrams, father and son, and their colleagues: The discovery of a new world, with all the astonishment, the widening horizons and the alteration of the world picture, was operative in their century as it had not been since the Renaissance.

The theme which had served as a lever toward
political, religious, economic and philosophical
revolution in the Renaissance was to work in new
fields engineered by men who believed they had only
to discover the laws of nature in order to bring order
and sanity to the earth.

Old conceptions, blurred by superstitions and dread,
were to be brushed off, turned about in the light and
named.

The times called forth originality, courted diversity,
called upon men to think and roam and to stand up for
their conclusions. Love of country did not exclude the
world.... The blood flowed around the world in sacred
wood sap and in the seeds of pine cones. For there was
a grand design at work; respect for the glory of
mentality.

If men could not conquer death, they might manage
life. All the monstrous, unmanageable things that
men had not known what to do with this side of their
experience, how to tame it, how to face it, this group
accepted in its most benignant aspect of sheer wonder,
unsolved miracle, potent might which might be bent to
man's salvation. It was a period auspicious for such a
breathing space; a time, for once, of decision and calm,
a hopefulness casting so strong a ray that all the violent,
the incomprehensible, was for a brief spell kept at bay.
(Pause) New Green World, you see, was written as a
kind of rescue work for myself, for it was during the
McCarthy period, when I felt so sunk, that I decided
to recall the intransigent Bartrams and their group of
wonder workers. A time when the fabric of knowledge
and being seemed not only continuous, but as newly
woven, perfect, almost.

By the time I finished the book, deep in the cold war,
and long after the events here narrated, the very real
war in Viet Nam had devoured legions of names,
and the fabric of order and system. At Dien Bien Phu,

Vo Nguyen Giap who had discussed the kid's text
book, *A Short History Of American Democracy,* with
our O S S boys at Pac Bo, had defeated the French once
and for all. That was in 1954,

the year *New Green World* was published.
   The French were out, the Americans were in. *(Pause)*
A lot of this is factual *(the fabric's torn);* but all of it is
true. *(She goes out.)*

(We hear HO CHI MINH *before we see him, behind him the
platform is bedecked in white and red. The people on the
platform wear white suits with neckties, and no hats, except*
HO CHI MINH. *He wears a high-collared khakitunic and
a wicker hat.)*

HO CHI MINH: All men are created equal. The creator
has given us certain inviolable rights; the right to life,
the right to be free, and the right to achieve happiness.
(He stops short.) Do you hear me distinctly?

CROWD: *(Roars back:)* Yes!

HO CHI MINH: These immortal words are taken from
the Declaration of Independence of the United States
of America in 1776. In a larger sense, this means that:
All the people on earth are born equal: All the people
have the right to live, to be happy, to be free.

(Slow fade to black. Lights up on the SECOND O S S
OFFICER *and* HO CHI MINH, *as before at Bac Bo palace.)*

HO CHI MINH: I must say that I am apprehensive of
the future. would like to know, even on an informal
basis whether you have any idea what American policy
towards Vietnam will be, especially in light of France's
obvious intention to return.

SECOND O S S OFFICER: All I know is that President
Roosevelt has on numerous occasions stated a policy of
no American support for French colonial ambitions and
no interference in the internal affairs of Viet Nam. The

policy's still operative, as far as I know.

I will go one step further to tell you that since the President's death no official statement by the United States questioned French Sovereignty over Viet Nam; but neither has the United States supported France in any postwar plans for Indochina. As a matter of fact, I know of no change in policy that requires the United States to assist France to reestablish by force its pre-1940 position in Viet Nam. The position of the United States could change if the Vietnamese people wanted the French to return under one condition or another. However, this is only speculation.

HO CHI MINH: You understand, then, my confusion regarding the precise nature of American policy intentions?

SECOND O S S OFFICER: I think you are aware of my personal inclinations.

HO CHI MINH: Yes, I am. We all are.

SECOND O S S OFFICER: However, my instructions just before departure for Hanoi and repeatedly since then have been that American representatives in Viet Nam are to be absolutely neutral.

HO CHI MINH: I understand what you are saying.

(Pause)

SECOND O S S OFFICER: Irrespective of my personal inclination for or against a particular group or cause I have to adhere strictly to my instructions and perhaps at times my actions may have been misinterpreted by the various interests.

HO CHI MINH: It is difficult for me to reconcile the United States position in Washington, Quebec, Teheran, and Potsdam with its passivity in current developments in Saigon—where pro-French and royalist elements provoked violence during the Independence Day celebrations.

I cannot understand how the United States, a champion of Anticolonialism can step aside and permit England and even China to assist France in its aim of reimposing colonial rule on Viet Nam.

SECOND O S S OFFICER: That is not our policy, as far as I am concerned.

HO CHI MINH: One would have to be blind not to recognize the fact that French troops, armed and equipped with American supplies, will soon attempt to reenter Laos, Cambodia and even the places they call Annam, Tonkin and Cochin China. *(Pause)* It will cost them dearly if they do.

But if only the United States would exert its influence with de Gaulle a modus vivendi could be reached in Viet Nam in which not only the French, but all friendly countries could benefit from Vietnamese independence.

(Pause)

SECOND O S S OFFICER: I am curious; what made you decide which political, political path was the correct one for you?

HO CHI MINH: At my early party meetings there was heated discussion on such questions as participation in the Second International, the Third International, the Workers of the World Movement, and whether our Socialist party should affiliate with Lenin's Third International.

I raised the naive question: which international sided with the colonials. A kind soul whispered. "The Third", and handed me a copy of Lenin's *Theses on the National and Colonial Questions*.

But how wrong we were ever to believe that the French, British or Russian communists would concern themselves with the Vietnamese problem.

When I was fifteen my father moved to Hue, and

I attended school there. I became deeply offended by the Western attitude of the Headmaster, and some of the teachers. And later, on my first visit to Marseilles I found the usual seaport derelicts, gamblers, smugglers, prostitutes. But the French people of Marseilles treated me kindly, while back home the French treated the Vietnamese with arrogant condescension.

Later I traveled to Portugal, Italy and Spain. I saw several West and North African ports and visited the Congo and Madagascar.

Everywhere I went I observed the attitude of the white man toward the Asiatic or African black. It was the same in Viet Nam.

How sad.

SECOND O S S OFFICER: I should be going. It's getting late.

HO CHI MINH: Carry back to the United States a message of warm friendship for the American people. I want Americans to know that the people of Viet Nam would long remember the United States as a friend and ally. We will always be grateful for the material help we have received, but most of all for the example the history of the United States has set for Viet Nam in its struggle for independence.

(HO CHI MINH *walks with the* SECOND O S S OFFICER *to the door, puts his hand on the American's shoulder.)*

HO CHI MINH: *Bon voyage.* You are always welcome.

(Black out)

(End of scene)

epsilon

(Back at O S S Headquarters. The O S S men are preparing to move back to China, thence presumably to the U S A.)

(Silence. We hear the wind blow. Silence)

(Pause)

(Both O S S men become thoughtful and very still.)

SECOND O S S OFFICER: What's that?

FIRST O S S OFFICER: What? What's what?

SECOND O S S OFFICER: I don't know. Thought I heard something. *(Pause)* I don't know what I'm supposed to do now. Say,*
   Have we got a copy of the Declaration of Independence anywhere around here?

FIRST O S S OFFICER: *(Hasn't heard)* What's that?

SECOND O S S OFFICER: The Declaration of Independence. Have we got a copy of the...

FIRST O S S OFFICER: *(Still hasn't heard)* How's that?

SECOND O S S OFFICER: Skip it. Just a little distracted.

FIRST O S S OFFICER: Probably the fatigue.

(Wind blows, fluttering the white cotton curtain, very high up. Both look, see the window is open.)

(Both stare at the window.)

FIRST O S S OFFICER: This came in while you were bidding a fond farewell to Uncle Ho. Straight from the desk of General Donovan.

SECOND O S S OFFICER: What is it?

FIRST O S S OFFICER: Our superiors in Kunming and Chungking. They evidently have a somewhat different picture of things here. Take a look at this.

SECOND O S S OFFICER: *(Reads aloud)* "...O S S field representatives in Hanoi report the Provisional Government to be politically immature, misled by Japanese agents-provocateurs and communist elements, and inclined to use words like 'liberalism', 'democracy', and 'nationalization' without understanding what they mean..."

FIRST O S S OFFICER: One of my pals in Kunming thought we should be aware of the fact.

SECOND O S S OFFICER: But this isn't what I reported. What is this?

FIRST O S S OFFICER: This is what Donovan reported to President Truman, based on your reports.

SECOND O S S OFFICER: But this is not what I have been reporting.

FIRST O S S OFFICER: That's the point, isn't it?

SECOND O S S OFFICER: What exactly do you mean?

FIRST O S S OFFICER: Isn't the inference pretty clear, Major?

SECOND O S S OFFICER: I want to hear from you exactly what you think the inference is. And what our "pals" in Kunming want us to be aware of?

FIRST O S S OFFICER: Cool down, Major. Cool down.

SECOND O S S OFFICER: But this is not what we have been reporting; this has no basis in the political and social reality we have observed.

FIRST O S S OFFICER: —

SECOND O S S OFFICER: What? What!

FIRST O S S OFFICER: Don't be obtuse. Policy is changing, evidently.

(Pause)

SECOND O S S OFFICER: This is pure hubris. This is the hubris of the French. And when they're finished. It will be our turn.

(Black out begins.)

FIRST O S S OFFICER: Did I hear you correctly. Were you looking for a copy of the Declaration of Independence? Did you want their Declaration of Independence or our Declaration of Independence? Because if you wanted our Declaration of Independence we don't have one on the premises...

(Lights out on our O S S boys.)

(Lights up on JOSEPHINE HERBST who returns downstage.)

(Pause)

JOSEPHINE HERBST: Let me quote: "Informant T1 stated that HERBST at one time wrote a story for a magazine, name and date of the publication presently unknown, wherein she wrote: 'I went down with a bunch of farmers in Bucks County, Pennsylvania, not far from where Washington crossed the Delaware, and voted a straight Communist ticket.

"Informant stated that JOSEPHINE HERBST has a violent temper, a revolutionist attitude, and has caused trouble wherever the opportunity presented itself. She is described as having the utmost contempt for the American form of government and for the so-called American 'liberal'" ...Well, I sure as hell do now, ah and this:

"HERBST is also known to have attended the scenes of several mid-west milk strikes ostensibly as a union helper".

That gives you an idea of the tenor of the thing, and

from time to time all during the fifties the accusations
kept popping up. But, as I mentioned before, I was
unable even to discover the nature of these charges
for years and years. Colonel Donovan, as I have also
mention before, was uncooperative, though it was he
who had ordered my firing.

Of the seven points listed in the document offered
by informant T1, in Reno, Nevada, six have reference
sources linked to Katharine Anne. My good friend,
Katherine Anne Porter. Now, of course, I never learned
anything about this till long after I was dead. And it's a
good thing, because there would have been hell to pay.

When Katherine Anne and I finally did break it was
over totally different matters: her reneging on a
promise to review my last full-length novel, *Somewhere
The Tempest Fell*, when it appeared in 1947; and also
her silly and misguided attack on Gertrude Stein in
Harper's, for which I could never forgive her. In 1962,
her last novel came out; the book was not very good
but it became a bestseller. In it there is not only no
lovemaking, but no fornicating worthy of the name.
There is only one Jew on board, and he is a classic
stereotype. There is no historical specificity, only a
generalized postwar sense of gloom and doom. The
book was called *Ship Of Fools*, and I sometimes feel like
we all got on board. My career sputtered on thanks to
a few, good friends. I was on the panel for the 1968
National Book Awards and talked straight through
the ceremonies.

The Colonel Donovan who fired me, and the General
Donovan who our boys in the O S S in Hanoi had to
contend with are one and the same. William J "Wild
Bill" Donovan. Won the Navy Cross, the Distinguished
Service Medal and the Congressional Medal of Honor
in the first World War. A war hero and attorney. A man
like that must know what he's doing, mustn't he?

I died in January 1969; Ho Chi Minh in September of

the same year. We lost the war six years later; fifty-five thousand dead on our side, over a million on the other; three trillion dollars of debt. And what good ever came out of it? *(Pause)* The Measuring Stick. That is the place to quarrel, not with what the Measuring Stick measures; certainly not with defending myself at all. *(She goes out.)*

(Blackout)

END OF PLAY

www.ingramcontent.com/pod-product-compliance
Lightning Source LLC
Chambersburg PA
CBHW070032110426
42741CB00035B/2735